AF272502

Publisher: BoD · Books on Demand GmbH, In de Tarpen 42,
22848 Norderstedt, bod@bod.de
Print: Libri Plureos GmbH, Friedensallee 273, 22763 Hamburg

first published by BoD, 2025
cover artwork ©Maxi Weimann
ISBN: 978-3-7693-5755-4

LORE VAIN

withering the velvet cloud
poems

to the people that inspire me

for half of a lifetime
we learn to
built a mask,
to mind feelings
not accepted
but to feel
is not a good bad thing
getting back to be true
not to be irritated
not to feel ashamed
and then to feel ashamed
but not to feel bad
about being ashamed
but to feel bad
and feel good about it
and not always being good
when someone asks you

how you feel

the storm abates
>but we barely speak
>>the blood we´ve bled
>leaves a picture in every street

>where new strangeness begins

we weep and sceam
>while birds keep singing
>>and the moon expands to full

i can hear your blood in my veins
>you can taste my pulse on your tongue
and we kiss

i killed the characters
into which i have hatched
a fitting mask for every matter
now it matters to be me
feeling love got me restless
it´s just there
in it´s excistence
i learn to swim

> direction was to the ground
> the buoyancy is low
> seem to merge with the sea
> no breathtaking
> then faint to dream
> and the darkness inside me
> is endless down there

realizing pain
the light breaks the surface
and the water breaks the light
you watch them dancing
each to the other
belongs but stays on his side

letting them tears dry
i did not let them die

this solitude is a place you don´t know
you closed the room
to loose the key
and much later opening it again
being sad about empty files,
only windows to the sea

first date felt like a movie
and you couldn´t take me home with the walls too thin
so we walked my way kissing on every red light
I said hold my hand a thousand times again like in that night
your face I painted on repeat, you threw me all the stones, I
did build a house and settled in
so each of your stones makes me feel vulnerable home
while you don´t believe I really wanted us to be

I ran into your bold ego
      it was leaning at the door
      of your insecurity
      too confident to feel empathy
      it was chewing the
      cheesy mistakes you did
      with an expression of contempt
      it spewed out sentences
      which I disliked
      and I wondered
why you let it rule
the polity of this door
knows no other call
than presumption

a blurry image you capture
and it says nothing
it only talks to the one
with a face so true
know we belong

don´t forget to change the film
before you go to sleep
talking your fear
with a tongue   you do

seen the moon
playing chess
the rook walking the square
all in blue

and I´m afraid too

all the mystery
that surrounds us
with an echo from the past

couldn´t hide the tears
and let us fall to feel what we must

if you posess me,
if you make me obsessed
could you just be the same

these nights I spend without you
seeing your face in the icecube
and drinking down
our endless memory

the smell of my wallet
       reminds you on your youth
              and we watched the crossaints in the sky
              while others call it the orange moon
little phrases I saved from the talks we had
       and I do remember it was special
              it was something to keep
you always left too early
and you had reasons to
I learned not to wait for words
       nor things to do
the only tension you set me into
was not to know any place
that could be replacing
this liaison with you

I was the one flying while you tried to make me walk
I was the one diving, when you tried not to drown
but I loved every move with you
and still wish we had more of those days to

late afternoon
went to the park

and we were talking
and breathing, the air fresh

still warm

I remember the grass and the lights reflections,
the eyes were one

but we also had a heavy theme collection
from now on

walked in between
we did not mind the gap

but I trust in that strong love
that grew rootless, unfounded, all wild in itself

these shadows proof i excist
while the night eats them up
I walk away from the light
letting my thoughts grow
thinking on you
and your
restless occupation
          of my heart
I listen to songs
you´d send me
and melodies
that never let me
go
a microdose theory
that never lets you
go

fleeting weakness of mine
when I see you entering the room
surroundings loose their shine
and I loose my words for you
as if they were meaningless
rather should have kept them
as treasures for the fickle ecstasy
on the table they roll like bullets
feels light
feels heavy
feels insane
must have met you on the moon
to feel so far
october doesn´t taste like summer anymore
I discovered your soul
and I uncovered mine
but now dare to shut down
shoot all them bullets
into the damn blue sky

it was only a dream
baby
only a dream

and you lost it

i kissed you in the shadow of your doubt
you kissed me feeling you´re not allowed

hoping you miss me
on your easy way out

but i know you would hate me to say that
cause you suffer from inside

the same time
we´re not living
in the same time

I keep him far from
where my love grows
it´s in a valley
called the false ground
it´s melting colors
like the clocks of Dali
where it never rains now
all insured in anxiety
we said we can´t move on
and I told you the truth
I will move all my heart
to another galaxy,
the one unreachable
I´m already on the way,
passing dried flowers
of last summer,
still rampant
when there was a
you and me

all words fail
they can´t form the silhouette
of what this

we never learned from
the past in war
suffer did not grow the brain
to anywhere
a simple change
doesn´t break through
while we drive fast
in the cars that
make us feel new
old rusted nails we run into
spending days
stranger
to the world we are born into

afraid of your words
I´m still longing to hear them
                    what might be moving your soul
only a suggestion

                    even the words,
                    what could they tell
                    I deny to open my eyes
                    but see the flickering lights
                    in a place that time forgot
                    I dream to walk these streets
            in the night
with you by my side
tell me things that make us
feel more safe in this world
only by forming a smaller world
that feels warm and soft
no matter the other
the outside was never inside enough

colorful mind
where you´ve been going to
losing your way?
and your moves
slowly slide from romance
trying too much
losing too much
to feel nothing at all

fragile love
come rip my heart out
try to give it someone I don´t know
push your fears out of the window
woun´t you look at me
while you look into the mirror
both sides suffercate your heart
I hear your scars talking
and you mess reading the cards
while walking
the stars fell in one lonely night
now you never talk straight
thinking of us
as something dangerous
I let you fade into the dust

a simple change
it doesn´t break me
of lazy lovers
I had enough
now burning down
I don´t want to
we were more
and you were more
a fire yourself
felt headed all the time
and left me
with the need
to let down
my everything inside
then I sold my heart
to the scattered,
a pattern in a bus
told me to stop tears
to fall from the ground
but they fall
while I´m on fever
they fall
while I´m cold
they fall even louder
when I try to hold

slave to the chain
that´s held in my hand
i want to lay me down
and feel nothing human
to feel like I´m not someone
but my foolish heart
keeps rubbing the dirt
in the cut

a thousand pieces
you die me in

it rains shiver
 from a velvet cloud
  I dreamed of a sailor
   to carry me out
    of my mind
     out of this humbled world of
      emptiness
       it rains darkness
        from a velvet cloud
         I´ve seen too many failing
          where it´s about to feel love

I planted the idea so deep into my heart
that the roots nearly broke it
waiting a decade for a message or a sign,
something meaningless maybe
until I´d fade into total loneliness
you´d chose one color of mine
to make it your favorite one
but why´d you dare to steal it
to get it back it took so long

you look different in pain
but I love you all the same
give me tenderness back
let me taste life to the fullest
like we once had

once there is someone
who got you there
you await the messages
you dare for him to care
and never enough
should tell you only one thing
if that´s all he got
you got his all
and you don´t feel anything
this cannot be something
it´s nothing to dare

too many thoughts
kept me from being creative
but ever since you left
I have an ongoing drill to write
and draw and I do sing out loud
I might have lost an idea
for the reason
we met
why
we met
might be reason
I again got lost in ideas
I do sing and draw and find out
that art is holding my hand in this love
all you can give is nothing for now
and it´s just enough if we had
the pure us to keep
from failing

thinking of you
in every face surrounding me
thinking of you
whisper words of poetry
-oh your words of poetry

restless thoughts on a train

seen every station in berlin
and still haven´t found its charme

but if you want me to be a piece of art
don´t cut me into pieces

bite me tender
just don´t eat me up

dirty daydreams
are alway a good idea
to steal some time from yourself

it´s just another digi star falling

I hope you call me
and drown me in your sound
I know nothing more vibrant
and nothing more silent
than your love to stick around

a light on your street
keeps me blind
and runs me out of your mind

every break in our conversation
,makes me fear
,you gonna fear

meeting someone
you´re unpatient to see again
got the best talks
and the most magnetic moments
meeting someone
you want to grab and melt with
all the time
that gives you pictures
you dare to hold
and that is not just
like everybody else
meeting someone
that makes you cry and feel
like you never been closer
you want that person so much
that you decide just to let go

every day
feels different
and what you know
is only about the yesterday
but this could be
a different day
and it might differ from all your days
you just walk outside
and it smells different
it tastes different
and not even looks
the same
like every day

I know we gonna meet again
and it fears me
I think about the right mask to put on
but there is not a fitting one
only the ones of the past
that already grew old,
their eyelids hang to the knees
and their mouth stays shut
since the dust layed down on them
I make up a stragedy
to form a new mask,
I ran out of material,
we don´t feel matere no more
don´t know your habits
anymore
how do I read what you
adore
do I even still want you to adore?

I
kindly
risk
to
be
hurt
feel
bad
again
when
I
over
and
over
scrawl
through
pictures
loosing
time
on
past
life
that
runs
through
my
fingers
life
runs
through
my
fingers

a swallowed foot
on sipping ground
these shadows ate all colors
rising without a sound

my skin, my soul I´d throw all in
the monsters stranglehold
I formed a poem to be told
on my clock you´re just a spin

a microdose theory
to make me forget you
but only for the night
these shades proof I exist
while I lost my mind
the other day we kissed
and listen to melodies
that never let me go

I´m in the valley
of the wild ground
driving fast
It´s melting colors
doesn´t know time
it´s way too exciting
for a dead boring life

contact software
you still excist in my dreams

~~I want to write you~~

I stay strong.

words are ghosts
and follow me
through the corridors
of our fallen out remembrance
it leads me nowhere
and everywhere
you
hopefully
never get there

I´m fire

don´t think you can only use my shine
running circles while you´re trying
to forget desire

heartache
I don´t know what we do
can´t get along with you
no more, no more

heartache
i don´t know this is cruel
I´m writing songs on you
no more no more

going though withdrawl
I´m on fever, suffer,
I think,
I overthink

I would love to heal with you
to be there for you
but honestly need you
to be there for me too

I would love to write with you
tell my secrets to you
that I die for you
every step you take away from me

I would love to hold you
staying silently awake with you
my heart racing for you
and all the things that we do

would love to tell you I miss you
instead I write all these lines about you
trying to find you
in every strangers face

the first one I miss so bad
       my concept of loss doesn´t work
           seems with every day
      you try to be forgotten
I miss you twice as much
      wearing the perfume
          that makes me remember
      want to meet you at eight
on the unknown place

letting go
passing by
and I need you
but I learned how to play
empty pockets
empty hearts
after burning
and we burned down
a lot

the haze lies on the fields
where I let my eyes fade
into the grey landscape
I can see pictures grow
deep in the unknown
I hope for nothing
but the past to repeat
what a nightmare
will I ever awake
and was I ever dreaming
fooled by the lights
that slowly rised in the back
off the surface
that falls apart
in the backyard
into thousand pieces
seeds to the ground

as fleeting as the scent,
which i hoped to linger

like every kiss
    every touch
    every tenderness

some things remain the same by changing

remember the days when we met
when we were close

a fragrance that accompanies you
when I wander between the planets
looking for infinity

I do not want to
kill my love
let it wither
put it in the corner

my way will therefore
never be yours

two
the word is so true
wrapped its arms around me
all summer
eternal rotation
while I remember hearing
cold phrases running down
the chest

useless
forget us
you don´t need me
so you can´t deceive me

a soft dystopia
two

tried to make friends
with the rainfall
but he went to sleep
on the velvet couch
where a kind whisper
tells stories about spring
the skin connects
with the soft surface
and the difference
between
forgetting
and
pushing away
slowly awakes

awakening weakness
eats them all up
with the notification
that loosing,
wishing and hoping
is not enough

so if spring might come
the rain might fall for it

there was fire in the air and a dizzy light
in the city of our own confusion
we became strangers for a little while
silent notifications everywhere
and the way you looked at me
was in a way that it was never meant to be
only the night could give a touch of salvation
and a quite agree
all of the tension grew from real love
and all this was a journey for both of us
I did not want to leave the boat
that was sailing so wild and free
did not even realize it made you seasick
for a good reason to be
and the hole year was burning
every ground we touched started turning
changes broke in
and every heart was breaking
that´s when winter came,
cooled down the scene
and the million broken heart shards
started to assemble anew

in these memories of daylight
I am shutting down the blinds
your face is displaying
on the walls of flickering lights
did not take heed
on my surrender
so it was a gift retracted

stranger,
you keep my heart in permanent danger
I drank you down
but I´m still thirsty
never planed to grow up

as fleeting as the scent

the sun almost rising
I never want you to go
but the cruel sky
doesn´t leave a doubt
we need to write
another chapter
another day
and leave them all
to an open end
the reader will hate us
the cartharsis is left to the greek
in our world
emotional tension
doesn´t lead nowhere
doesn´t heal from the seek

you wear my favorite skin
I wanna touch it all the time
you might fool your heart
I woun´t let you fool mine

this little park in the rain
it became a magic place
for the things we´re sayin
the lights reflection
enlightening the dark water with perfection

the color of your voice
known so well
there was not even a choise
the weeping willow
is now holding the secrets under it´s pillow

waking up the next day
under chaotic stucco in a way
I feel us, we´ll be ok
and since a long time
this left me feeling sublime

do you come from prose or poetry
an arrow hitting the sky slightly
how lovely the risk
and how deep the cut
an inch from here
you did never not
trust to heal through desire
going all in on fire
now to leave that flame
a distant shout turns into eternal game
the arts hold their hands
promise them to never sleep
since the night dances in a beautiful cocoon
you forgot it all and won´t leave too soon

-scalpel en velours

we met surprisingly
made the night our stage and ran
up and down the corridors
changing faces, loosing scores
and we yearn endlessly
even your heart is folded
I long to be in it
I want to melt with it
and we run free
and I will never hold
I let you go
but I hold on
my love

we changed so many words
the silence now makes us strangers
but it feels to be the only chance
to put us back in romance
somehow our clouds driftet apart
and I can only keep you in art
but the current you cause in me
is the strongest to feel
it´s the only one,
the only that felt so real

I sink in the deep room of writing
  it is a place to disappear
  and to rise with the stories you burn for
    it requires the failure
    the fingers touching the wrong keys
    and live with a dissonance
      the ashes offer new soil to grow
      and to be more
    than a repetitive lyre of folk songs
    there´s no need for oblivion
  let´s not become meaningless
  no hiding in empty envelopes
and for the tension not to fail
      hire the swinging metronome
      the surreal pendulum of infinity

taking your time